LEO'S BIG DREAM

A Story About Money, Dreams and How to Build a Future

Written by: David J. Hernández

LEO'S PLAN — PART 1

www.leosplan.com

Disclaimer:

The information provided in this book is for informational and educational purposes only, and it is not intended to be used as professional advice. While the content is inspired by real-life events, the characters and situations are fictional. Any resemblance to actual persons, living or deceased, or real-life events, is purely coincidental. This book is not intended to provide legal, financial, or other professional advice, and you should seek the counsel of a qualified professional before implementing any information or strategies mentioned here. Results may vary depending on the individual and their specific circumstances. David J. Hernández is a licensed real estate broker, and his opinions are his own, His opinions, as represented in this work, do not represent the views of any real estate association or company he is affiliated with at the time of publication.

AI-Generated Content Disclosure:

All of the images in this book were generated by Gemini. Three of these images were then slightly expanded using Canva's Magic Extend feature. The original material was primarily authored by the author, David J. Hernández, with subsequent editing, additions, and refinements made with the assistance of ChatGPT and Gemini to enhance readability and clarity for a broader reading audience. The material was also updated to stay close to our current real-life timeline.

ISBN: 978-1-970954-01-2 Library of Congress Control Number: Pending.
Printed in the United States of America

DEDICATION

This is dedicated to every kid who's ever heard: "we can't afford it" and they still dared to dream.

To all the parents who have felt the pain of not being able to give more to their kids.

For everyone who was told: "you can't do it" and they went and did it anyway.

To my mother, Berta, for her love, faith, strength, wisdom and perseverance.

To my immediate family, my extended family and all my good friends.

To those who have inspired me and have influenced my life, because their life lessons did matter.

CONTENT

ACKNOWLEDGEMENT

I would like to thank all the people who took time out of their lives to read the early versions of this book and provided feedback to help me get to this version.

Their sharp eyes helped me tremendously to keep this work simple and grounded.

I also want to thank my family for their endless patience during the late nights I spent in front of my computer.

WHY I WROTE THIS STORY

Money is confusing — especially when you're a kid.

Most of us didn't grow up knowing how money worked, or how businesses or rental buildings worked, or how rents could turn into a financial opportunity. Most of the people we knew were renters, like us. Some of them moved often. Some of them really struggled to get by.

For many families, there was never a conversation about making money in any other way than through hard physical labor. In some cases, that's all some of our parents knew.

This story is for families like ours, who had to work really hard for everything we have now.

It's for kids who notice things.

For parents who want something better for their families, but don't always know where to start.

For teachers and community leaders who believe we have to plant the seeds early on.

This story is not about getting rich quickly.

This is about learning, being smart and understanding how money works.

It's about starting early to build a legacy for your family.

It’s about realizing that ownership isn’t just for “other type of people.”

With the right guidance, information and strategies, we can all build lasting wealth.

This story is for you.

And I hope this is only the start of something bigger.

— **David J. Hernández**

Leo's Big Dream

CHAPTER 1

LEO WONDERS ABOUT MONEY

Leo Castillo sat on the front steps of his house, swinging his legs while playing with a pebble in his hands, and watching his neighbors carry grocery bags to the building at the end of the block.

He wasn't thinking about school.

He wasn't thinking about cartoons.
He was thinking about something way more confusing.

Money.

He whispered to himself: "Why does it seem like grown-ups are always worried about money?"

His mom had smiled that morning, like always — but Teresa's smile didn't quite reach her eyes. His dad, while rubbing his temples, said: "We'll figure it out." Leo didn't know what they were trying to figure out.

But he felt the pressure and noticed how the anxiety was creeping in his mom.

The bills were piling up again.

And then, his best friend Lucas. His family had just moved less than two months ago — the second time in two years. He remembers it well because they moved just a month before Leo had turned eleven.

Leo's family owned their home — a small single-family house on a busy block, with an affordable mortgage payment — but they still talked about money like it was a ghost. Always there, always haunting, never enough.

He threw the pebble towards the front of the house, where there was a bed of white pebble rocks and a row of decorative bricks.

Leo had heard different people complain:

"Why is rent so high?"

"Why can't we stay in the same home for more than one year?"

"I don't want to leave my friends again and start over."

"There isn't enough money."

He heard these phrases before — from Lucas, from some of his other friends, from his own family — and they felt like echoes in his head.

That's when he heard a voice call out.

"Hola Leo! Come here mijo!"

It was tía Rosa, standing by her car, keys jingling in one hand and a paper bag in the other.

"I got conchas." She said with a grin.

Leo jumped up. "Coming!"

He liked tía Rosa. She always had snacks. And she never talked down to him. She just got him.

She handed him a round sweet bread covered in a sugary paste that made it look like a seashell and she smiled.

"You're thinking about something?"

Leo nodded. "Just... stuff."

Tía Rosa raised an eyebrow. "Leo stuff? Or family stuff? Is it about money?"

Leo's eyes widened. "How'd you know?!!"

She chuckled. "Because when I was your age, I was the same way. I used to watch my parents whisper about bills too. I didn't understand it all back then, but I felt it — just like you do now. And I see you also wanting to help your parents."

Leo bit into the bread and mumbled through crumbs, "How can they work so hard and still always be worried?"

Tía Rosa nodded slowly. "That's a good question, mijito. And I think it's time we talked about it. But not all at once. One story at a time. Deal?"

Leo grinned. "Deal."

Leo didn't know it yet, but that was the day everything started to change.

CHAPTER 2

THE HOUSE THAT SLIPPED AWAY

There was a time when Rosa Burgos thought she had done everything right.

She had a husband, Pedro Gómez. She had kids, Santy and Lily. She had a house with a little yard and a tree that leaned just enough to look cool in pictures.

It wasn't a fancy house, but it was theirs.

People said: "You did it! You're living the American Dream!" And she really believed she did.

Until it all fell apart.

The crash came in 2008. At first, it just felt like a few bumps — prices going up, her husband working longer hours. But then it got worse.

The value of their home dropped, and the payment went up. Her husband would argue with her all the time, and one day he stopped coming home. And the bills... they didn't stop coming; they did not stop for anyone.

Rosa tried to save it all. But in the end, she lost the house by the end of 2010. The bank took it, and the house took away with it her pride, her peace and her sense of safety.

She and her kids moved into a small apartment, and they struggled to get by. And for the first year, she just survived.

Until one day, while folding laundry, she heard a podcast she was playing as background noise, something about multi-unit buildings.

She paused, hit replay, and listened to it again.

She said out loud:

"Wait... You can buy a building... live in one of the apartments... and rent out the rest?"

It sounded like magic. But it wasn't. It was math.

That day, at the end of January 2013, Rosa started her second life.

She found classes about real estate, homeownership and getting investment properties. She started asking a lot of questions. She met other people who had done it, new friends, who looked just like her.

By the end of 2013 she was finally divorced and ready for this new stage of her life.

She learned about loans made for first-time buyers, grants and other assistance programs.

She never knew any of this help was available when she and her ex-husband bought their first home.

She also learned about buildings with three and four units being treated almost like regular houses by banks.

She didn't have much... but she had just enough money saved to make it work. And she had the right people around her to guide her.

She bought her first 4-unit building with an FHA loan at the beginning of 2014. She lived in one unit. Rented out the other three.

And for the first time in her life — the rent paid the mortgage, and she had money to save. She could breathe again.

But she didn't stop there, she kept learning and bought more buildings.

She made good friends with her advisors, and became especially close with David Hernández, her real estate broker, and Martín Puerta, the priest who opened the church's doors for seminars to help people keep their homes, even though that didn't work out for Rosa.

Now Rosa has three buildings. Not because she wanted to be rich... But because she never wanted to be powerless again.

Today, years later from the crash, she looked at Leo — smart, curious, feeling things in his heart he couldn't quite name yet — and thought:

"Maybe I can save him some time."

Not to rush him. Not to push him. Just to plant the seed. And water it, little by little.

Chapter 3

A Building That Pays You?

Later that week, Leo sat with tía Rosa at her kitchen table. She poured him a glass of mango juice and set out a plate of sliced apples with chili powder.

"Okay," Leo said, licking some chili powder off his fingers. "Tell me again. You bought a building... and people live in it... and they pay you?"

Tía Rosa nodded. "That's right. I live in one unit, and the people in the other three units pay their rent. Those rents cover my mortgage payment."

Leo blinked. "So, wait… you don't pay for your house?"

Tía Rosa smiled. "Nope. My building pays for itself. I just manage it and I take care of the units, so the people who live there stay happy and pay me their rent."

Leo's eyes got big. "That's like a cheat code!"

Tía Rosa laughed. "Not really a cheat code, just a smart move."

Leo asked: "But… isn't that, like… for rich people? My parents aren't rich. We could never do something like that."

Tía Rosa leaned in. “Leo, I wasn’t rich either. I was broke when I started. But I found a loan that helped me buy a building with just a little bit of money for the down payment.”

“Like how little?” Leo asked, narrowing his eyes.

“Three and a half percent,” she said.

Leo scrunched his face. “Is that a lot?”

Tía Rosa chuckled. "Not compared to the whole price of the building. It's like buying one slice of pizza but getting to eat the whole pie every day."

Leo stared at her. "Wait… what?!!"

"Okay, maybe not the best example," Tía Rosa said, laughing. "But the point is that it's doable. You don't have to be rich. You just have to learn the right steps."

Leo leaned back in his chair, staring at the ceiling. "Why don't other people do this?"

Tía Rosa's smile faded just a little. "Because it's scary. Because it sounds complicated. And because no one ever told them that this is possible."

Leo thought of his parents. How tired they looked. How hard they worked.

He looked at tía Rosa. "Did you tell my parents about this?"

She responded softly: "I did, but they were nervous. Francisco said it wasn't for them. That it sounded too risky."

Leo whispered: "Yeah, they always say they don't want to take chances and put us in a bad situation. They say God will provide."

Tía Rosa nodded. "Sometimes fear sounds like logic. But really, it's just fear in a fancy outfit. God can give you the tools, but we have to decide if we use them or not."

Leo didn't say anything for a while. He just looked at the juice glass in his hand.

Finally, he said: "I wanna learn how to do it. Not now… but someday."

Tía Rosa reached across the table and squeezed his hand.

"And that's why I'm telling you now, mijo. So you know it's out there. So when you're ready… you'll already have the map."

CHAPTER 4

A NEW WAY OF SEEING THINGS

The next day at school, Leo couldn't stop thinking about what tía Rosa said to him.

His teacher was going on about fractions, but all Leo could see in his notebook was a big number: 3.5%.

He wrote it down. Circled it. Drew a little building next to it.

He imagined one apartment with a dog barking. Another with a grandma making soup. One with a baby crying. And one with him and his family — not worried, not whispering, just… chill.

He looked up. Everyone else was solving a word problem about bananas. Leo smiled and thought: "They have no idea."

After school, he walked home past a row of buildings. Some had peeling paint. Some looked brand-new. He started counting the groups of windows.

"One, two… three… four. Four units. Just like tía Rosa's building."

He started guessing: “Rent’s probably like… $900 for each apartment. That’s $3,600 a month!”

He paused. “Is that enough to pay the building and the bills?”

He didn’t know. But he wanted to know.

Leo pulled out his phone and searched on the website tía Rosa used with David: “How much does a 4-unit building cost in Chicago?”

The numbers scared him a little. But they also… excited him.

At dinner that night, he stared at his parents while they talked about groceries, the mortgage payment, his mom's student loan, the bills, and needing new tires for the car.

He wanted to say something. But not yet.

Instead, he washed the dishes and went to his room.

He opened his notebook and wrote across the top:

"Things I Need to Learn:"

- What is a mortgage?
- What is a loan?

- What makes a good building?
- What is a down payment? Tía Rosa mentioned that.
- How much money do we need?
- What does tía Rosa wish she knew when she started?

He underlined the last sentence twice and whispered... "I'm gonna ask her that tomorrow."

CHAPTER 5

WHAT ROSA WISHES SHE KNEW

The next day, Leo sat at tía Rosa's kitchen table with his notebook open. He flipped to the page where he had written:

"What does tía Rosa wish she knew when she started?"

Tía Rosa was slicing mango and adding lime and salt, just the way Leo liked it.

He cleared his throat. "Tía Rosa, remember when you said you learned all this stuff the hard way?"

She nodded.

"Well… what do you wish you knew back then?"

Tía Rosa smiled and sat down across from him. "Whew, that's a long list."

Leo held up his pencil. "I'm ready." 

She thought for a moment, then said, "I wish someone had told me that fear sounds like logic. That just because something feels scary to us, it doesn't mean it's wrong. It might just be something new for us."

Leo wrote that down. 

Then she said: "I also wish I knew how powerful a 4-unit building really is. Let me show you."

She grabbed a napkin and drew four little boxes. 

"This is a 4-unit building. One for you to live in. Three you can rent out."

"Wait! so I live in one, and the rent from the other three… pays for the whole building?!" Leo said.

Tía Rosa winked. "Exactly! 😉 You don't have to be rich. Just be smart."

"That's like having roommates who pay for everything!" Leo grinned so hard, it hurt a little.

Tía Rosa laughed. "That's one way to put it."

She pulled out another napkin and scribbled three little houses. 

"This is what I wish I knew about the available choices in condition of the properties," Tía Rosa explained:

Home A: Move-in ready. Costs the most. Usually already finished and needs no repairs or updates. These homes often have multiple buyers competing for them. Sometimes you overpay for them.

Home B: Needs some work or updating. Costs less. These homes might sit there on the market longer, and you may be able to negotiate a better price or get money back.

Home C: Needs a lot of work and can't be purchased with a regular loan. These homes cost the least because they need a lot of work, and they might stay in the market the longest. You may also be able to negotiate a better price or get money back.

Tía Rosa whispered. "But guess what? Home C has the most secret treasure."

"Treasure?" Leo leaned in. 

Home A: Move-in Ready

Home B: Needs Work

Home C: Hidden Treasure

"**Equity**. That's the money you make after you fix it up. Like buying an old house in bad shape, fixing it, and selling it for more. You get your money back — and you get some more — because of the value you added when you fixed it," said tía Rosa.

"Okay, very cool. I like fixing things. And I love treasures."

Tía Rosa continued. "Now, let's say you want to buy one. But you don't have a mountain of money."

Leo nodded. "I don't even own a bike that works!"

She smiled. "That's okay. Banks have tools called '**loans**.'"

She made a small chart and explained:

First-Time Buyer Loans: An FHA loan requires just 3.5% in down payment, and a Conventional loan requires at least 5%. Both options are great for people who are buying for the first time. Very affordable when you don't have much money.

FHA Loan: This is great when your budget is tight, or your credit isn't perfect, or you have more debt than you want. They have some more strict requirements.

Conventional Loan: This may give you access to grant programs and other Assistance that FHA does not. They have different requirements.

Credits: FHA also lets you get more help from the seller — up to 6% in credits for closing costs. Conventional usually limits the help to 3%.

Renovation Loans: This is when you have to fix or upgrade the place you are buying. This loan wraps in the cost of the house plus the repairs, one loan, one payment.

VA Loans: Loans with 0% down payment for veterans or active military.

Future Rent Money Counts as Income: If your building has rental units, the rent you expect to receive can help you qualify for a bigger loan.

Grants and Assistance: Some banks, cities, or states offer help with your down payment or closing costs. We'll ask my broker about those when the time comes, because some programs have an end date, others run out of funds, and others just get updated every so often.

Gift Money: Even grandma or other family members can help if you're short on savings!

Leo's eyes sparkled. "That's like building a castle with borrowed building block pieces!"

"Exactly. And there's more," she said, sliding over another napkin.

She laid out the numbers and the notes like they were puzzle pieces.

If you buy a Condo or a House: you pay for absolutely everything by yourself.

If you buy a 2-Unit: your renter helps you pay the mortgage, but you still need to pay a lot from your own pocket.

If you buy a 3-Unit: your renters help you pay the mortgage, but you might still need to add a little bit from your own pocket.

If you buy a 4-Unit: your renters should cover the whole mortgage payment and the expenses. You might even have money left over. This extra money should be saved, and it can be used to cover unexpected issues.

"More units equal more money."

Leo did the math on his fingers.

"So… wait. I pay less to own more? That's bananas!"

"Yes!" "Bananas that grow into money trees." Tía Rosa laughed.

Leo raised an eyebrow. "So, it's free?"

"Not quite. In life, nothing is really free, you pay for everything, one way or another.

That's why you should pay yourself rent. Set aside the same amount you'd charge someone else if you were renting your unit to them — and save that money in the bank.

Avoid tricking yourself into thinking living there is free.

Make sure you pay yourself at least fair market rent — paying yourself less is like cheating on your own future."

Leo nodded.

"So… wait. I pay myself, save my money and my renters cover the building?"

"Exactly! That's the move!" Tía Rosa laughed.

Then Leo got quiet. "But what if the tenants don't pay?"

"You have to pick tenants in a smart way. Remember David, my Broker? He helps me get the apartments rented. ☺ And once they are rented out, you should keep as much money saved up as you can. Just in case. That's your emergency fund."

"What if I lose my job? Or what if the tenants lose their jobs?"

"The rents still pay the mortgage. You can always tap into your emergency funds, if it's really necessary. You'll have time to get back up."

"What if I mess up the repairs?"

"You hire people who know what they're doing. That's what grown-ups who know about this do all the time. They don't try to do everything themselves."

Leo nodded slowly, writing it all down.

Then she leaned in, in a gentle voice. "Leo, the world will tell you: buy a big house. Be the boss. Show off what you have. But that only drains your wallet. Do you want to know

what the real magic is?"

She tapped the table like she was knocking on a door.

"Buy smart. Build slow. Let others help you pay for your property. And one day you won't have to work — you'll be able to choose if you want to work.

And that... that's real freedom," she said softly.

Leo looked down at his notebook and wrote one more line at the bottom:

"I'm going to build my empire."

Then he looked up and smiled.

"I'm gonna do this," he whispered.

And tía Rosa whispered back:

"I know."

CHAPTER 6

COULD MY PARENTS DO THIS?

Leo sat in his bedroom with his notebook wide open and his brain spinning.

Everything tía Rosa said made sense.

The numbers. The buildings. The loans.

The way fear dresses up like logic.

He started thinking about his parents.

They were good people. Hard workers. The kind who made rice and beans stretched for three days without complaining.

But they never talked about owning buildings. Or rent paying for the house. Only about bills. And stress. And maybe one day… if things got better, they'll be fine.

Leo chewed the top of his pencil.

"What if tía Rosa told them of all this?"

Parents' World

4-Unit World

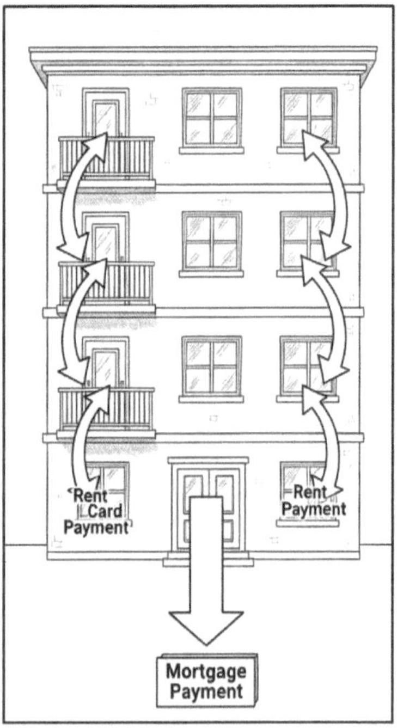

She said she already had. And they said no. Too risky. Too hard. Not for us.

But, what if they saw that they weren’t that different from her?

Leo remembered what tía Rosa said. She had to take care of Santy and Lily. Uncle Pedro left them. She had a job that barely paid enough to survive. And still, she figured it out.

He wrote:

“Maybe they just need to hear it again. From someone they trust. Or maybe… from me.”

He looked at the numbers again — the 4-unit setup, the low down-payment, the idea that rent counts to qualify for a building, so that’s why it is better to get as many rents as possible.

It wasn’t magic. It was a strategy.

And maybe, just maybe, if he learned enough, he could be the one to explain it in a way they could understand.

Because tía Rosa already had the knowledge. His parents already had the work ethic.

He whispered to himself: **“I just need to build the bridge.”**

Then he smiled and added something to the top of his page:

Mission: Help my parents buy a 4-unit building.

Mission:
Help my parents
buy a 4-unit building.

Chapter 7

Not Yet!

Tía Rosa arrived and sat at the kitchen table with Leo's parents.

Leo sat quietly nearby, notebook in his lap, pretending to doodle while listening closely.

Tía Rosa had her folder open, papers spread out like a little special road map for them to use.

She had just explained how a four-unit building works. One unit to live in. Three to rent. Rent helps pay the mortgage and allows you to save money.

Leo had already heard this — but hearing tía Rosa say it to his parents made it feel different. Bigger. More Real.

His parents looked at each other. Teresa raised her right eyebrow, and Francisco squinted his eyes just a little bit for a few seconds. Then they looked at the numbers on the page again.

Francisco said: "We already have a mortgage, wouldn't that stop us from getting another loan?"

Tía Rosa nodded gently. "It might. Especially if the bank sees that most of your income already goes toward your current house payment."

"So, we wouldn't qualify?" Teresa asked.

Tía Rosa said softly: "Not unless you sold your house… or rented it out, that's the rule. The bank needs to see that you have room in your budget for the new payment."

Leo's parents got quiet.

Leo could feel it. It was that invisible wall going up again.

Teresa said: “We’re not ready to sell. This is our home. We raised Leo and Gaby here, and Leo is in school now. It’s not a good idea to move in the middle of the school year.”

“And renting it out feels very risky. What if it doesn’t work out? What if we have to pay two mortgages? We can’t afford that,” Francisco added.

Tía Rosa didn’t argue. She just nodded.

She said: “It’s okay. You don’t have to do anything right now. But if you ever change your mind, or if you want more details, you know where to find me. I’ll always be here with you, we are family.”

They all sat in silence for a moment.

Leo looked down at his notebook. He felt something heavy in his chest — it was not disappointment exactly, but it was something similar.

Later that night, after tía Rosa had left and the dishes were done, Leo sat on his bed.

He opened his notebook and flipped past the numbers and boxes and napkin math.

He found a blank page.

At the top, he wrote:

“Keep learning.”

Then underneath:

“Even if they’re not ready.”

He glanced over at Gaby’s room. She was still a toddler now — just learning how to hold a crayon.

Leo smiled to himself and added one more line:

“One day, I’ll teach her too.”

CHAPTER 8

LEO'S BIG IDEA

Leo sat by the window the following night, notebook open, head resting on his hand.

The moonlight spilled across the page, but he didn't need light to see what he was thinking.

He'd been thinking about it all day.

His parents weren't ready.

But maybe someone else could be.

He flipped to the page with the boxes and napkin math.

Then he grabbed a pencil and started writing a new question at the top:

"What if someone else could do it?"

The next day at school, during lunch, Leo sat next to his friend Lucas.

They talked about the usual stuff — homework, their teacher's weird socks, and how cafeteria pizza tasted like regret.

But then Lucas said, “My parents said we might have to move again. The owner just told them rent is going up $300 in a few months. We can’t afford to pay that much.”

Leo blinked, “Again?”

Lucas nodded. “Third time in two years.”

Leo looked around, leaned in, and said, “can I show you something?”

Lucas shrugged. “Sure.”

Leo pulled out a folded piece of paper from his backpack.

It was his drawing — the one with the four units, the arrows, and the math.

Lucas stared at it. “What’s this?”

"It's the way my aunt bought her first building. She lives in one apartment. The rents from the other apartments pay the loan," Leo said.

Lucas's eyebrows went up. "Wait… you can do that for real?"

"Yeah, and it's not just for rich people. My aunt started with almost nothing.

She learned how it works. And also, there are programs that help with the money you need to start," Leo said.

Lucas leaned in. "Can my parents talk to her?"

Leo smiled. "I was hoping you'd say that."

That night, Leo opened his notebook and added a new note:

“Help Lucas’s family talk to tía Rosa.”

It wasn’t the plan he started with.

But maybe… it was the beginning of something even bigger.

CHAPTER 9

PROOF IT WORKS

A week later, Leo sat on the front steps, from where he could see tía Rosa's property.

He was paying close attention and felt a little anxiety, while he was waiting for something.

Lucas and his parents were walking up the sidewalk. They looked nervous. Curious. His mom, Bertha, had a folder in her hands. His dad, Andrés, had questions in his eyes.

Tía Rosa had stepped out onto the porch. "You must be the Carril family," she said with a warm smile.

Lucas smiled. "Tía Rosa, these are my parents."

Tía Rosa shook their hands, led them inside, and offered them coffee, juice and cookies, like she always did. Then she pulled out the same folder she had shown Leo's parents a few days before.

Leo didn't go inside. He didn't need to.

He already knew what she was going to say.

He sat on the steps and watched the street. Kids rode past on bikes. A man walked his dog. The sky was soft and blue.

Two hours later, the door opened. Lucas and his family came out — not smiling, not celebrating... but talking. They were starting to take in everything they had discussed with tía Rosa.

Lucas looked over at Leo and gave him a quiet nod.

Leo nodded back.

Two weeks later, Lucas told him:

"We're going to apply for a loan. We're looking for a 4-unit building with mister Hernández, tía Rosa's broker."

"For real?" Leo's eyes lit up.

Lucas grinned. "Yeah. My dad said we wouldn't even have thought about it if you hadn't said anything."

Leo didn't know what to say. He just stared for a second, then said: "I'm happy for you. This is awesome!"

That night, Leo sat on his bed, with his notebook in his lap.

He wrote:

"Lucas's family is buying a building. This actually works."

He paused.

Then he added:

"Maybe my family can do it too. Just not yet."

CHAPTER 10

THE LONG GAME

Days later, during the weekend, Leo went to visit tía Rosa again. It was just the two of them this time.

They sat on the porch with cups of lemon grass tea. The sun was starting to dip behind the buildings, and the breeze smelled like the neighbor's carne asada.

Leo told her everything.

About Lucas.

About his family.

About how they were really going for the building.

Tía Rosa listened with her whole face — nodding, smiling, letting him talk.

Then she said, "And how do you feel about all of that?"

Leo stared out at the street. "Happy. And… a little weird."

"Weird?"

"I guess I thought… I'd be first."

Tía Rosa nodded. "That's fair."

"But I also know it's not a race. It's about the right time. And right now... my family's not ready."

"Yet," Tía Rosa said, raising an eyebrow and lowering her chin a little.

Leo smiled. "Yet."

They sat in silence for a moment. Then tía Rosa reached into her tote bag and pulled out a small notebook — the kind with a soft leather cover and stitched spine.

She handed it to Leo.

"What's this?" he asked.

She looked at his eyes with a soft smile, and then she said:

"It's blank… but not for long. Use it to write down everything you learn. Your questions. Your ideas. The stuff you want to remember. And the stuff you want to share."

Leo flipped through the pages. It felt like it belonged to him already.

He wrote three words on the first page:

"The long game."

Chapter 11:

The Spark Spreads

A few weeks later, like almost every other school day, Leo sat at lunch with Lucas. The air was colder now, and most of the trees outside were starting to drop their leaves.

"Guess what?" Lucas said, barely able to keep it in. "We're under contract. It's a 4-unit building between my mom's job and our school, so I don't have to transfer schools and lose my friends."

Leo dropped his sandwich. “No way!”

Lucas nodded. “The bank confirmed we are good to go. And tía Rosa and mister David helped us understand the whole process.”

Leo grinned so wide it hurt. “That’s amazing!”

“I told my parents you were the reason we even started looking. They said to tell you… thank you. So... thank you brother, for real... thank you for helping us!” Lucas said.

Leo didn’t know what to say. He just blinked, then said, “I’m really happy for you. This is freaking awesome!”

That night, Leo wrote in his new notebook — the one Rosa gave him:

"Lucas's family is buying a building. It's not a dream. It's a real building."

He paused while thinking, stared at the page, then he wrote:

"My parents aren't ready. But I am."

He flipped to the next page and drew a little map.

One house.

An arrow.

Then, a 4-unit building.

He added a note:

"This is how we move forward. One step at a time."

He looked out his window. The city lights were blinking softly in the distance.

"I'm not waiting. I'm learning.

I'm not just hoping to be lucky. I'm planning.

I'm not just dreaming. I'm building."

CHAPTER 12

ONE DAY AT A TIME

The weekend after Lucas's family moved into their new building, Leo visited tía Rosa again. It was a bright and sunny Saturday morning, warmer than unusual for that time of year.

This time, he brought his new notebook, the one she gave him.

It was already half full — sketches of buildings, arrows, numbers, questions, and ideas he wasn't sure he fully understood yet.

They sat in the kitchen, sipping agua de Jamaica and listening to the soft hum of traffic outside.

"I heard that Lucas's family already moved to their new home," Tía Rosa said with a smile.

Leo nodded. "Yes! They're really doing this. God bless them."

"You helped them get there."

"I guess so, but I'm still just learning," Leo said, blushing a little.

Tía Rosa leaned over, opened a drawer, and pulled out an envelope. She handed it to Leo.

Inside was a folded sheet of paper. On the top, it said:

"Things I wish I learned earlier."

Below it was a list — short, simple, and full of wisdom:

Don't wait until you have all the money.

Start small.

Ask questions.

Take care of what you own.

Let other people help you grow.

Build slowly, build smart.

Be good to your tenants.

Keep your word.

Write things down.

Don't forget who you're doing this for.

Leo read it twice. Then he folded it up and tucked it into the back of his notebook.

"What is this?" Leo asked.

Tía Rosa said: "Seeds, plant them when you're ready."

Leo smiled.

That Sunday, after mass, his house was full of people and different smells.

His dad was grilling carne asada in the yard. His mom was making lemonade in the kitchen. Gaby ran around chasing bubbles and tía Rosa sat on the porch with a paper fan and a cold drink.

Even Father Martín stopped by for a while after his last Sunday mass. David also stopped in after his open house.

It wasn't a holiday. Just a good day, warm and sunny. Perfect to spend time with the family.

Leo sat at the picnic table with his notebook. His cousins were laughing. His uncle was telling the same story he always told. And Leo? He was writing.

He wrote on a little calendar, circled a few dates. He made a checklist for summer. He even sketched a new building: one with space for his family, and extra rooms for friends.

Tía Rosa peeked over his shoulder. "Still planning?"

"Always." Leo smiled.

She nodded. "That's how it starts. One page. One step. One day at a time."

Leo looked around — at his family, his neighborhood, his little sister dancing in the grass.

He closed his notebook and whispered, **"One day, I'll help my parents do this."**

He held the notebook close to his chest and added:

"And, when I'm old enough, I'll do it too."

Then he looked up at the cherry blossom tree outside, topped by a bright blue sky, and said one more thing:

"In the meantime, I'll keep sharing what I know and what I learn — because somebody out there needs this, just like I did."

Leo's Notebook – Part 1

What I've Learned So Far

- A 4-unit building lets you live in one apartment and rent out the other 3.
- Rent from the other apartments can cover your mortgage.
- Loans like FHA (at least 3.5% down) and Conventional (at least 5% down) help first-time homebuyers.
- An FHA loan allows more seller credits (up to 6%), which helps if you have more debt or a tight budget.

-  A Conventional loan allows access to some grant programs that FHA does not allow.
- 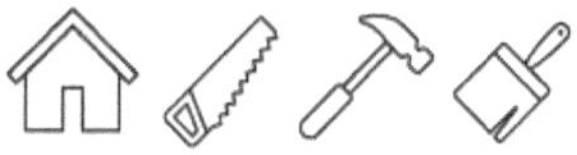 You can include repairs with a renovation loan.
-  You can count future rents as income to qualify for a higher loan.
- You don't need to be rich — you need the right strategy and the right information.
-  You should pay yourself rent, even if the building covers the mortgage and leaves you a profit. This will help you save money.
- Fear sounds like logic, but it's just fear in disguise.
- You can start small. You don't have to be complicated.
- Always ask questions.
- Be smart. Be kind and respectful. Keep your promises.
- If it doesn't help others too, it's not really building.
- Don't let greed get to your head, stay grounded.

- Surround yourself with professionals who will help you and guide you.
- 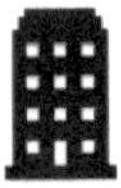 Learn what makes a good building.
- Read, learn, listen to podcasts, and go to classes.

Comparing Different Types of Homes *(What I Learned)*

What Type of Home? What Each One Means for Your Money

Single-Family Home

You live in the whole house.

You pay everything — the mortgage, the taxes, the insurance, the repairs.

No one helps you with the payment.

Condo

You own your apartment.

You still pay for everything, like in a single-family home.

Plus, you have to pay condo fees every month for shared stuff like the roof or the hallways.

2-Unit Building

You live in one apartment and rent the other one.

The rent helps pay the mortgage — but it only covers a portion, you have to put money from your own pocket for mortgage and bills.

Since it doesn't cover much, it takes a lot longer for you to save up money.

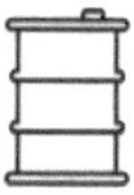

3-Unit Building

You live in one apartment and rent the other two.

The rent helps pay the mortgage — but you might still need to add some money from your own pocket for mortgage and bills.

It doesn't always cover everything, but it helps a lot to save up some money.

4-Unit Building

You live in one apartment and rent out the other three.

The rent should cover the whole mortgage payment and bills — and, if done right, you have money left over!

You can save up any extra money or use it for repairs.

Everything you save can help you to buy the next building.

In my opinion, this is the smartest way to start.

Important Tip: ***Be Smart and Pay Yourself Rent.***

That means you save money in the bank every month — just like real rent — avoid tricking yourself into thinking this is free.

Nothing is free. Make sure you pay yourself at least fair market rent. If you save that money, you're building your future.

Investing in your own future must be your priority. If you pay yourself too little, you're just cheating yourself.

What are the Best Types of Properties to Build Wealth?

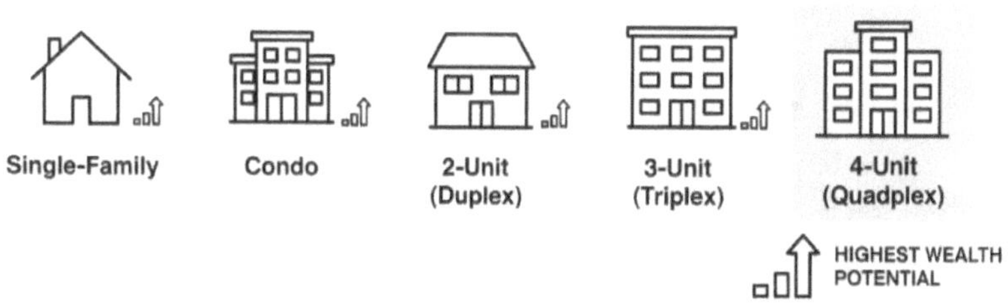

What is Equity? *(In Simple Words)*

Equity is the value you build in something you own.

Imagine you buy an old house for cheap because it needs a lot of work. You fix it up with new paint, floors, and windows. You redo the kitchen and the main bathroom. Then someone wants to buy it from you — and they pay a lot more than what you paid to buy it and fix it.

That extra money you made? That's equity.

Now, imagine you don't sell, you keep the house instead. The value still went up — so if you ever sell it or borrow money against it, the part that's "yours" when you compare the value of the house and what you owe, that's the equity.

When people buy old houses or buildings and fix them up to be worth more, and sell them, that's called a **flip**.

You buy they house; you spend money fixing it… then you sell it for more than what you paid in total. The **money** you get back **after paying off the bank loan and the costs of repairs, that** is the **equity** they built.

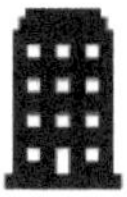 In a building you keep instead of selling it, as you keep collecting rents and you pay off the loan, your equity grows over time. As you reduce the debt and time passes, the value of the building keeps increasing.

 It's like planting an apple tree in the yard — it grows year by year.

The way it looked when you first planted it is totally different than what it looks like now. In the beginning it was small, it didn't have any apples.

Then seven years later, it got big, it gives you shade and apples. And even with the big storm last year that broke one big branch, the apple tree is still there.

All that tree growth is like the equity growth in a building.

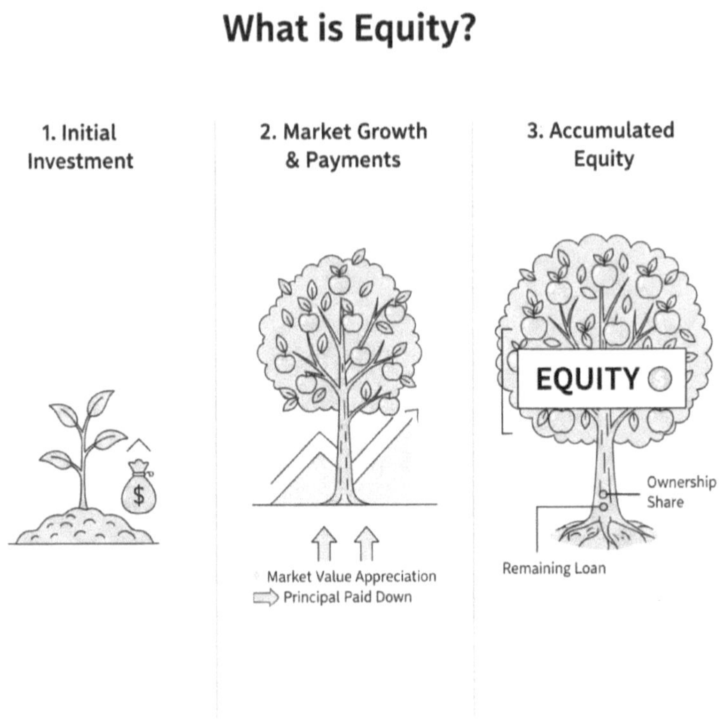
What is Equity?
1. Initial Investment
2. Market Growth & Payments
3. Accumulated Equity
$
Market Value Appreciation
Principal Paid Down
EQUITY
Ownership Share
Remaining Loan

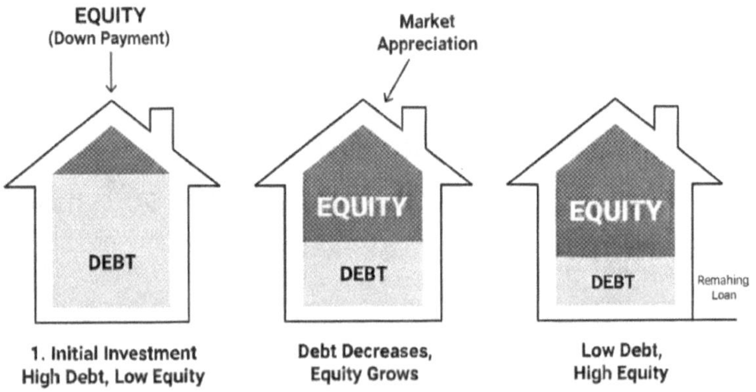
EQUITY (Down Payment)
Market Appreciation
DEBT
EQUITY
DEBT
EQUITY
DEBT
Remahing Loan
1. Initial Investment High Debt, Low Equity
Debt Decreases, Equity Grows
Low Debt, High Equity

FHA vs Conventional Loans *(When You're Starting Out)*

FHA Loan

- The down payment is only **3.5%**
- Great for people with **low credit** or **higher debt**
- Allows up to **6% in seller credits** to help cover your closing costs
- **Does not allow** certain grants or outside assistance programs
- **We can use future rental income to qualify**

Conventional Loan

- ✓ The down payment starts at **5%**
- ✓ We can qualify for **special grants and assistance programs** not allowed under FHA
- ✗ Only allows **up to 3% in seller credits**
- ✓ **We can use future rental income to qualify.**

There are different tools for the different needs of different people — but both loans can help you get started!

FHA Loan vs. Conventional Loan

	FHA Loan	Conventional Loan
Down Payment	3.5% Down	5-20% Down
Credit Score	Flexible Credit	Good Credit
Mortgage Insurance	Long-term MI	Removable PMI
Property Condition	Stricter Rules	Standard Rules

My Plan (Even If It's Not All Possible Yet)

Things I can do now:

- Keep learning — ask questions, take notes, pay attention.
- Watch how people treat money and how they talk about homeownership.
- Visit buildings and learn how to spot a good one.
- Practice "napkin math" — guess the rent, compare it to the costs.
- Help my friends if they need this information.
- Pay attention to my own money — saving even a little will help.
- Write down everything tía Rosa tells me.

- Learn how the grants and assistance programs work.

- Understand all the numbers I need to know and prepare for the different options.

- Find out what other expenses come with the building.

- Find out all the responsibilities of the building.

- Learn to identify the people who can help — the ones I need to know to be successful.

Things I want to do one day:

- 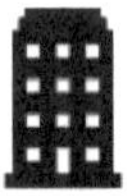 Help my parents own a 4-unit building
- 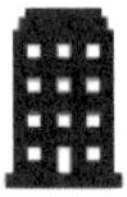 Buy my own 4-unit when I'm old enough
-  Build my savings little by little
-  Teach this to someone else who needs it
-  Grow slow and smart — like tía Rosa said
-  Turn this into something big for my future

____

____

____

____

My Plan

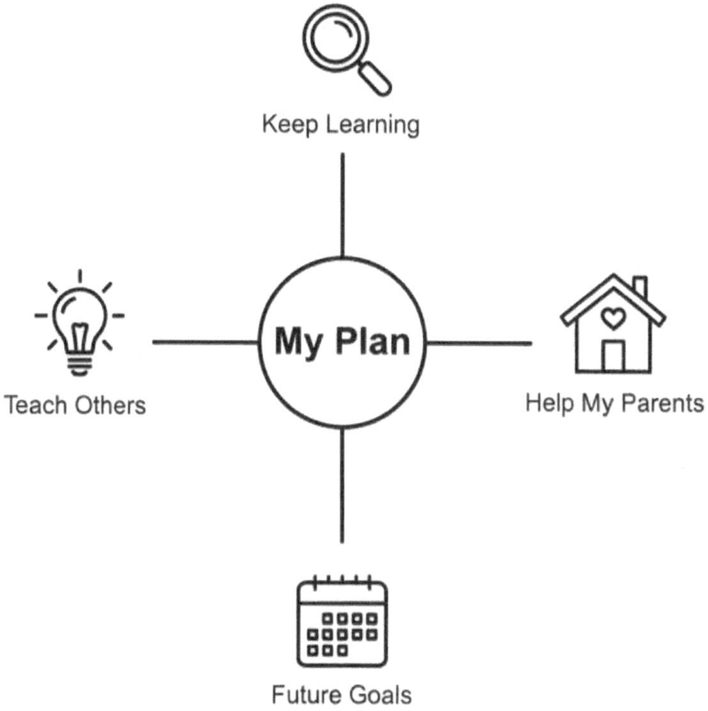
Keep Learning
Teach Others
My Plan
Help My Parents
Future Goals

BUILDING MY VOCABULARY – (PART 1)

Words I didn't know before, but now I do! Big ideas explained in simple words.

- **Mortgage** – A loan from the bank that helps you buy a home. You pay it back little by little each month.
- **Down Payment** – The money you pay upfront when buying something big, like a building.
- **Closing Costs** – The money you pay for the day of closing for the loan itself. They include the charges from the bank, the taxes from the sale and other fees.
- **Rent** – The money people pay every month to live in a home or an apartment.
- **Renter or Tenant** – A person who rents a place to live from someone else and pays that person rent every month.

- **Loan** – Money you borrow that you have to pay back later, usually in monthly payments.
- **Building with Units** – A building that has more than one place to live. Each apartment is called a "unit", each one is like a separate home.
- **4-Unit Building** – An apartment building with four places to live — you can live in one of them and rent the other three.
- **FHA Loan** – A loan that helps people buy a home with a small down payment — just 3.5%. In some aspects, this loan is more flexible than a conventional loan. It's great if your credit isn't perfect or you have more debt. FHA loans also let the seller help with closing costs — up to 6%. But many grants and assistance programs don't work with FHA loans.
- **Conventional Loan** – Another type of loan for people who are buying for the first time or who are buying a second home. A loan that requires at least 5% down. It's a good option if your credit is stronger. It also lets you use certain grants and assistance programs that FHA won't allow. With this loan the seller can only help with up to 3% of the closing costs.
- **Qualify for a Loan** – When the bank checks your money situation and says yes, you can get a loan.
- **Strategy** – A smart plan you make to reach a goal, step by step.

- **Closing** – The day you complete the purchase. It's when you sign the documents, you pay the down payment, and then you get the keys to the house.
- **First-Time Buyer** – Someone who's never bought a home before. The bank, the city or the state sometimes gives some people special help if they meet a specific program requirement. Ask David.
- **Using Rent to Qualify** – When a bank lets you use future rent money to help you qualify for a loan. In this case you don't need to have landlord experience for this to work. There are specific rules on how to use this rent to qualify.
- **Investment** – Something you buy that can grow in value and help you earn money later.
- **Grants and Assistance** – Somewhat free money or help to make it easier to buy a home. Some banks, cities, and states offer help for your down payment or closing costs. We'll ask David or the lender about those when the time comes, because some programs have an end date, others simply run out of funds, and others get updated every so often.
- **Risk** – Something that scares you because it could go wrong, but it could also be worth doing it. Like trying something new and, even though it scares you, you still do it because the benefit is bigger than the possible loss.

- **Napkin Math** – When you make a quick and simple math calculation to see if something makes sense. It's as easy as writing the numbers on a napkin, a piece of paper or a notebook, just to see if the math works or not.

- **Equity** – The increase in value of something you own. You can grow equity when your property becomes worth more. Depending on what your debt is now on that property, the equity is the difference between your current debt and the current value of the property. — Think of the increase in value when you own something and it goes up in price — like turning an old broken car you bought for cheap, fixing it and then selling it for a lot more. That profit you made, that's the equity.

- **Income** – Money you make from working, selling or renting something out.

- **To Be a Homeowner** – A person who owns a house, either because they bought it, won it or inherited it. The property can have a mortgage debt or it can be free and clear of debt.

A Note from Leo

Hi there,

When I was very little, my family moved a lot. Then we bought a house — but things were still tough. I started noticing that some of my friends had to move too, mostly because their rent kept going up and they needed to find cheaper places to live in.

I didn't like seeing that and I wanted to understand why it happened.

That's when I started learning from my tía Rosa. And guess what? I found out that even kids can start learning how money and rental buildings work. You don't have to wait until you're a grown-up.

Now I see things differently. I ask more questions. I take notes. I even talk to my friends about it.

Even if my family hasn't bought a building yet, I know one day we will. And I'm gonna be ready when the time comes.

You can do the same. Just keep learning. Keep asking questions. And don't give up. Write everything down, just like I wrote in my notebook everything tía Rosa shared with me.

If your family is going through something like this, just know this — you're not alone. You can learn, just like I did. You can be ready for the future.

If you're reading this and thinking, "Could I do that too?"

My answer is:

Yes, Yes You Can!

Your friend,

Leo Castillo

A MESSAGE FROM TÍA ROSA

Hola amiguita o amiguito,

Maybe no one has told you this before, but I will:

You are smart. You are strong. And you can help your family in big ways — even if you're still a kid.

Some people think grown-ups always have to be the ones teaching. But sometimes, it's the kids who lead the way. Like Leo. And maybe… like you.

You don't have to learn everything in one day. Just take one step at a time. Ask questions. Read. Write down what you learn. Talk to someone you trust. And little by little, you'll get ready.

I hope this story planted a seed in your heart.

Now go water it — but with actions.

Con cariño,

Rosa Burgos

A Message from David

Hola,

If you saw yourself in this story — even just a little — then I hope you feel what I felt while I was writing it:

That our lives are more than bills, or stress, or some unanswered questions.

That we come from families who know sacrifice and struggle, and we survive.

That we deserve more — and that we can build this "more" for ourselves with the right strategies and guidance.

This story isn't just some fiction. It's a roadmap.

It's inspired by real people, real neighborhoods and real decisions.

Maybe you're like Leo — ready to take your next step.

Or maybe you're like Rosa — ready to teach and share what you've learned.

Or maybe you're just starting, like Gaby — barely learning to see the world in a new way.

Wherever you are in your life, I want to help you.

This work is something personal to me. I've lived it, I've taught it and I continue to walk this road with families just like yours.

So, if you're ready to:

Learn more about real estate and homeownership.

Get support and guidance in buying your first home or your first building.

Or simply have someone in your corner to answer questions or brainstorm.

Reach out to us:

www.hernandezchicago.info

773-250-7590

Let's keep building. TOGETHER!

And if this story helped you or made you feel something — please pass it along to someone you care about.

Share it with a friend. A neighbor. A student. A parent.

Someone who needs a little hope, a little clarity or a little inspiration.

We’re not just helping people become homeowners — we’re helping them build their futures, one at a time.

With a lot of hope for all of us,

David J. Hernández

Creator of the ***Leo’s Plan*** Series

www.leosplan.com

My Notes

DAVID'S MISSION

David J. Hernández is a real estate broker focused on buying and selling real estate investment properties and has taught at several educational institutions. The core of his work is sharing investment strategies to build wealth. He has lived in Chicago for almost 40 years.

Growing up, David didn't learn much about how money worked, especially when it came to housing. Now, as an adult, he values more how hard working-class families worked, as they are the ones who need the most help. He understands why working-class people have to move so often, and how little people talk about homeownership. That has stuck with him as an adult.

Today, David has a mission: Help change that story.

Through his work and practical knowledge of real estate investments, David helps people understand how property ownership can create lasting financial stability and generational wealth. He is committed to sharing this knowledge with young people, minority families, and other communities that have been left out of these conversations for too long.

This story is part of a larger dream: to make financial knowledge feel less scary for working-class families; and for people to realize that they too can learn and use these strategies to build wealth.

David believes in the power of sharing stories to educate and inspire. But more than anything, he believes in planting seeds early on and helping others grow their seeds, overcoming their fear and limiting beliefs. He wants to help people take smart steps toward their financial freedom.

If you need to talk about housing, homeownership, how to invest in real estate or if you want to know where to start, **David is here to help.**

Connect through Phone Call, Text or WhatsApp:

773-250-7590

Or visit his Contact Page to access his website, social media, and other tools at:

www.hernandezchicago.info

About The Author

David J. Hernández is an author, who was a college professor for more than a decade, and has over 20 years of experience helping build financial stability through rental properties. His main goal is to teach families how money works so they can live with peace of mind. David grew up in a business-oriented family, learning that careful planning and hard work are the foundations for a life of self-improvement, prosperity, and fulfillment.

As a teacher at universities such as UIC, DePaul, and St. Augustine College, David learned to explain complex topics in a simple way. He created an easy-to-follow plan so anyone, regardless of their background or level of education, could improve their financial future through rental properties. David strives to make difficult things easy to understand by everyone. He takes confusing ideas about credit, savings and mortgage loans and breaks them down into simple steps that everyone can follow. He teaches his clients smart ways to become rental property owners, showing them how certain types of buildings can generate income to cover their own expenses and produce profits. This helps families financially, which reduces their stress levels. To be able to provide the best advice possible, he takes specialized courses and keeps up with real estate news.

David believes that when one person succeeds, the entire community benefits. One of his core beliefs is that we should treat others as we would like to be treated. He cares about helping the financial well-being of his clients and works to help other families prosper. He believes that everyone deserves the opportunity to thrive, grow, and choose to be a part of the light that illuminates the world. David was born in Perú, has lived in Chicago since 1989, and understands very well the challenges of working-class Hispanic families in the United States. His main goal is to share his knowledge with the families who need it most. He believes that sharing this information is the best way to empower the community and ensure their voices are heard.

Through his books and teaching style, David helps families and young people gain greater control of their finances and build a more powerful future than the one they expected, using rental properties to achieve their goals.

Made in United States
Troutdale, OR
11/03/2026

56844706R00080